# Soul Stories

Cover Photo by Sharon McCutcheon on Unsplash

Compilation, Editing & Lay-out Carol MacLennan,
Sheila MacDonald & Teri Crawford

*Thank you to Lila Robertson for the inspiration!*

Indian Edition

*This book is dedicated to the*

*Greatest Storyteller of all time*

*Some day you will be old enough*
*to start reading fairy tales again.*

# Our Story

The stories we tell, reflect the state of our hearts. We tell stories to entertain, educate and uplift. They remind us of our goodness and the goodness of humanity. Stories shine a light on the value of the small but significant heroics that make life worth living.

It is possible that there is only one story - the story of humanity's rise and fall. This same story is told in countless ways, in many languages, with unique and varied cultural symbols, but it is the same story. We lose ourselves. We lose connection with our goodness and then we find it again. During the dark times in between, we do battle with evil forces, demons and bad guys. In the end, it is always our goodness that wins.

*This series of stories is intended to tell a larger story, the story of humanity.*

Although some of these stories are well known, we have taken the time to catch the spiritual essence of each tale. Our attempt to elaborate the spiritual principle offered by the story is intended as a gift for each of us to use in our daily lives.

***This is our story, your story.***

***Enjoy…***

# The Human Spirit

The human spirit is filled with virtues.

Some of these virtues have gone underground, away from the surface of life where the negative and corrupt energies of the world threaten their goodness. Virtue seeks refuge in a wounded heart and shields itself with ego.

These stories remind us of the presence of virtue in the soul and the wonder of seeing them used again. The fact that these stories touch our hearts says much about our deep longing to fully experience our virtues again.

The good things in life, the things we long for - love, peace and happiness - have no pictures for us to use as a practical reference. We cannot see love; rather it is an experience, a feeling. The same is true for peace and happiness. However, the feelings and pictures associated with our lived experiences are stored as memories. Stories awaken these feelings.

When we remember something familiar, but forgotten, the longing to *come home* to the experience inspires us to create it again.

***We re-create what's known to our heart.***

# Renewal

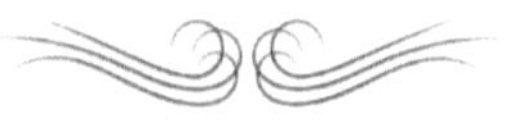

*As I change, the world changes.*

This has been the mantra of the Brahma Kumaris since the 1940s. Today we understand that the personal is global. We know how the flapping wings of a butterfly in one part of the globe can affect the weather patterns in another place. We understand that collective consciousness has created the world we live in and that a shift in individual consciousness can influence the world. We are interconnected.

At a personal and collective level, our world is shifting. We are witnessing changing patterns in our social, economic, climate and political landscape which require us to adapt and change.

Now, it is time for a renewal of consciousness, because...

*We have lost the plot.*
*We have put the material before the spiritual.*
*We see this reflected every day in the world we have created.*
*Now is the time to restore spirit to the heart of all things.*

But what precipitates the change of consciousness required for us to change the way we think, the way we live and ultimately change our world?

Personal and planetary crisis propel us to ask questions and examine ourselves with an eye to change. The shift in consciousness that follows, in turn leads to new behaviours. Then, in the blink of an eye, a ripple of change is created which, in time, transforms the world.

Collectively, we already share a common picture of what a better world can look like. When asked to describe their idea of heaven or a better world, most people (including those who do not believe in heaven) describe a similar place. It has a lovely clean environment, everyone is treated with respect, everyone is safe and cared for and we all live in peace.

These stories are meant to inspire faith in renewal and highlight the virtue-based actions that will transform our world. Each story contains an element necessary for our renewal as a human family.

*Once a group of villages decided to pray for rain. On the day of prayer, all the people gathered.*

*But only one boy came with an umbrella.*

***That is faith.***

# Being Ordinary

The sun smirked in the sky, daring my shoulders to resist its fiery heat. As I pulled the bowstring back to brush my cheek, I could sense fifteen sets of eyes watching me in rapture. I breathed in and released my fingers; the arrow whizzed through the air and sunk deep into the target. Bull's-eye. As I turned towards my audience fifteen little hands shot into the air, begging to be chosen first.

I knew nothing about archery when I arrived at camp, but a few hours a day guiding over-excited children taught me all I needed to know. The kids who didn't know me as their counselor referred to me as 'the archery girl'. One boy was so taken with the session that he painstakingly crafted his own bow out of a little stick and a piece of twine. He carried it around in his walker all week. Every day he begged me to take him to the archery range, oblivious to the fact that I had my own group of little girls hanging off me. On the very last day, when I found a few spare minutes to test it with him, I knew the result would be disappointing. Sure enough, the arrow dropped off the bow and landed a few feet from where he'd released it. I turned to him with my best supportive, 'good try!' face, but he just shrugged his shoulders unperturbed. Matter-of-factly he told me that no good bow-maker could expect success on their first try. The whole walk back to the cabins he chattered on about his ideas for modifications.

That summer I witnessed hundreds of similar moments. Each kid had his or her own story, interconnecting and overlapping into a distinct whole. Camp is meant to make kids feel extraordinary, and they do - whether it's making a bow and arrow, steering a canoe, or building a fire. Wearing a superman costume to every activity is common practice. Racing to finish eating chocolate pudding with no hands is applauded. At every meal many voices would routinely yell: "CAMP IS GREAT, ALL THE TIME!" as if affirming the only truth known to humankind. And most of the time it felt like it was true.

In the vast appendix of hilarious moments, one in particular stands out. It happened on a week that I'd been assigned a cabin of six young boys. They bounced off each other like charged atoms, always ricocheting into a new stratum on the spectrum of trouble. But every time I thought I'd reached my limit - I just couldn't dismantle one more booby trap - they'd look up at me with huge toothless smiles, and I'd somehow find the energy to painstakingly cut down the suspended teddy bears and toothbrushes. This reserve of energy was no small feat, especially at bedtime when the summer heat and their combined energy made sleep near impossible – for them, and by default for me.

One morning – after a surprisingly calm night – I went into the boys' room to wake them up. As I pulled on the covers of one bed, it became increasingly obvious that the boy cocooning inside, Ben, was not going to budge. When I finally coaxed him out, the others snickered knowingly as I tried to hide my shock, the front half of his hair had been haphazardly cut off. Patches stuck out at different lengths like a badly mowed lawn. Despite my instincts, I managed a stunned smile to counter his pout, and cheerily said, "Ben if you're the first one ready I'll give you a piggyback to breakfast!" That magic sentence wiped all thoughts of the haircut from the boys' over-stimulated brains, and I was left to confiscate the scissors and sweep up the discarded curls.

It took one piggyback ride and a breakfast of burning curiosity before Ben pulled on my hand and pointed to his hair, whispering ashamedly, "I was too hot last night." That and his signature pout were the only explanation anyone got for his new hairdo. But by the end of the day, we'd contacted his mom and evened out the chunky back section of his curls. After jovially convincing him that it wasn't a big deal, even he started to laugh. That night at the staff meeting, multiple retellings turned the haircut into a camp urban legend. Even now anytime I reminisce with fellow counselors about that summer it usually begins with: "Remember that week when Ben cut off his hair?"

A haircut wasn't the only unpleasant surprise I had to deal with that summer. A few weeks later, one of my older girls, Emmy, had a particularly difficult relationship with the water. Usually a chatterbox, she spent most of her time dancing around the cabin and asking me if her sequined hat matched her Betty Boop yoga pants. But when it came to swimming, she became mute and wouldn't put more than her feet in.

Then one day as I sat with her on the wharf, she started talking about conquering fear. The origin of the conversation confused me, until she glanced at the water and whispered that she was scared of sharks. Bolstered by her confession, I explained that there were no sharks in lakes, and offered to help her overcome her fear. So, we buckled her into a lifejacket, and I began to coax her down the ladder. After three successful rungs, she froze and shook her head. Watching from the water, her cabin mates cheered her on - but she'd hit an invisible wall and refused to go any further that day.

That first attempt began a painstaking week of cajoling her limb by limb into the water. Everyday I'd float on a flutter board and use every positive reinforcement technique I could think of to convince her she was safe. Other staff would periodically take a turn, hoping they'd be able to fulfill their counselor-ly desire to see a kid succeed. The best attempt was by a lifeguard named Claire, who tempted Emmy with the prospect of a ride behind the sit-atop kayak. This got her further into the water than any other day, and it was her last chance. As she calculated - her finger swirling uncertainly in the water by her thigh - a sweet smell infiltrated my nostrils. I looked around to locate the source of the stench and saw the other councilors crinkling their noses too. One of them motioned subtly to convey what I hadn't yet realized: Emmy had peed herself. Her distress had caused a physical response. I could see in her eyes that the imaginary sharks petrified her, but she was determined to face her fears.

When we finally left the waterfront, long after another counselor had taken the rest of my cabin back, Emmy started to cry. She reached for my hand and sobbed about how she couldn't make herself get in the water, even though she wanted so badly not to be scared. I squeezed her hand and reassured her that she'd done her best, distracted for a minute from my desire to get her into the shower. But before we could get to the cabin, she wrapped her arms around me and said she loved me for helping her. The smell of her internal struggle clung to my clothes for the rest of the day.

Anyone who has been to camp can relate to stories of archery, pranks, and swimming. We've all chanted things like "camp is great, all the time." But this particular camp isn't about making normal kids feel extraordinary. It's about making extraordinary kids feel normal, often for the first time in their lives.

The boy with the bow and arrow had never seen one before and to this day he still hasn't: he is blind. I taught him to shoot by guiding his fingers and playing music behind the target. By beveling it with hot glue, I made sure he could feel the bull's-eye when he hit it.

Ben cut his hair off because he was too hot, but also because he had Attention Deficit Hyperactive Disorder, and Oppositional Defiant Disorder. His mind did not have the capacity to warn him that cutting his hair might not be the best course of action. And his cabin mates were constantly fighting because between severe anxiety, Turrets, OCD, and autism, they could barely find a common denominator to co-exist, let alone have fun.

As for Emmy, she had Down syndrome. A disease I still know little about. I'm impressed all over again every time I think of her standing in her pee-drenched lifejacket, struggling against her own mind. Although lake-sharks seemed ridiculous to me, she was determined to overcome a very real phobia.

That summer I learned more than I've learned in three years of university. I know what an ostomy bag is and how to put in a feed-tube. I can deal with a severe asthma attack calmly. I've listened to a sixteen-year-old matter-of-factly describe the sixteen heart surgeries she's had. I've watched a nine-year-old with a leg amputation shoot three bull's-eyes in a row. I've seen a boy refuse to go swimming because his best friend's white blood cell count was too low to risk getting in the water. And I've played Quidditch in the pouring rain with 30 kids suffering from juvenile arthritis. Afterwards more than half of them told me it was their new favorite sport.

At camp I learned that every "no" can be a "yes." Every limitation is just a challenge to overcome. Although, in reality, camp isn't great all the time - it can be the most exhausting, trying job in the world – for some, it's the greatest life has to offer. I realized that being extraordinary is more tiring and disheartening than I can ever understand. And sometimes the chemotherapy and open-heart surgeries and tumor removals just are not enough. Sometimes all a kid needs, is to be normal.

*Rachel Morgan*

*It is a paradox of spirituality that one can be extraordinary on the inside, shining with the treasures of virtues and self-awareness, yet on the outside be very ordinary in the eyes of the world. Spirituality is an adventure in a direction opposite from the material-minded, external display of today's world. The focus of spirituality is to generate and cherish high quality internal energy. The true vibrancy of every human is the qualities and virtues they bring to living.*

***The beauty of the soul can be seen with an observant eye.***

## The Window

A young couple moved into a new house.

The next morning while they were eating breakfast, the young woman saw her neighbor hanging the washing outside.

"That laundry is not very clean. She doesn't know how to wash correctly. Perhaps she needs better soap powder."

Her husband looked on, remaining silent.

Every time her neighbor hung her washing out to dry, the young woman made the same comments.

A month later, the woman was surprised to see a nice clean wash on the line and said to her husband, "Look, she's finally learned how to wash properly. I wonder who taught her this?"

The husband replied, "I got up early this morning and cleaned our windows."

*I see the world through the window of my mind.*

*My mind is a precious place. It will be filled with the energy I allow inside. It can be like a temple or a dustbin. Sweet, kind, appreciative thoughts fill my mind with beautiful energy. When I understand that I have the power to determine the quality of energy in my mind, I will allow entry to only those thoughts that fill it with beauty. The world I see around me will reflect the view in my mind.*

***Cleaning the window of the mind improves the view.***

# Hospital Bed

Two men, both seriously ill, occupied the same hospital room.

One man was allowed to sit up in his bed for an hour each afternoon to help drain the fluid from his lungs. His bed was next to the room's only window. The other man had to spend all his time flat on his back.

The men talked for hours on end. They spoke of their wives and families, their homes, their jobs, their involvement in the military service, where they had been on vacation.

Every afternoon, when the man in the bed by the window could sit up, he would pass the time by describing to his roommate all the things he could see outside the window.

The man in the other bed began to live for those one-hour periods where his world would be broadened and enlivened by all the activity and color of the world outside.

The window overlooked a park with a lovely lake. Ducks and swans played on the water while children sailed their model boats. Young lovers walked arm in arm amidst flowers of every color and a fine view of the city skyline could be seen in the distance.

As the man by the window described all this in exquisite details, the man on the other side of the room would close his eyes and imagine this picturesque scene.

One warm afternoon, the man by the window described a parade passing by. Although the other man could not hear the band — he could see it in his mind's eye as the gentleman by the window portrayed it with descriptive words.

Days, weeks, and months passed.

One morning, the day nurse arrived to bring water for their baths only to find the lifeless body of the man by the window, who had died peacefully in his sleep. She was saddened and called the hospital attendants to take the body away.

As soon as it seemed appropriate, the other man asked if he could be moved next to the window. The nurse was happy to make the switch, and after making sure he was comfortable, she left him alone.

Slowly, painfully, he propped himself up on one elbow to take his first look at the real world outside. He strained to slowly turn to look out the window besides the bed.

It faced a blank wall.

The man asked the nurse what could have compelled his deceased roommate who had described such wonderful things outside this window.

The nurse responded that the man was blind and could not even see the wall.

She said, "Perhaps he just wanted to bring you both joy."

*True sight is the ability to see with the eye of imagination. Life comes alive when I can see between the cracks of the physical world to the rich inner world of the spirit. I can see beauty anywhere when I am attuned to this subtle vision.*

***True seeing is done with the heart.***

*Story telling is the most powerful way to put ideas into the world.*
Robert McKee

# The King's Favourite Elephant

A King had many elephants, but one in particular was very powerful, very obedient, very skillful and had the best fighting skills. Many times, he was sent to the battlefield, and he would return only after being victorious. He was the most loved elephant of the King, out of hundreds and thousands.

A time came when the elephant became old. He was not sent to the battlefield anymore but was still loved and part of the king's team. Whenever the king saw him, he felt good, he felt happy.

One day, the elephant went to the lake for a drink, and he got stuck in the mud. He began to sink. The more he tried to get out, the more stuck he got. He couldn't get out. He began to call for help.

The people knew he was in trouble by the sound of his screams. The news also reached the king. The people were in a panic because everyone knew he was the king's favourite. When the king reached the lake, he saw a lot of people gathered around the elephant. They had made many efforts to get him out, but they could not move him, and he was still stuck.

After some time, an old, retired minister of the king's court passed by. He suggested to the king that he have the battle drums played around the lake. The listeners found this bizarre, but as soon as the drums started playing there was a change in behaviour of the troubled elephant.

The elephant slowly pulled his massive body up into a standing position and ever so slowly pulled himself out of the mud. Everyone around him was shocked. They had thought he was too old and weak to get out of the mud, but it wasn't a lack of physical ability in the elephant, just the will to make the effort. The drums instilled the will and a feeling of enthusiasm, and then it was done.

*When I firmly commit myself to something with a pure intention, I become unshakeable. A true commitment has determination within it. Without commitment, excuses will arise and distract me until I give up. Life will test my commitment but if I stand firm, eventually the challenges will give up. Victory is based on determination.*

***Anything is possible when the will is awakened.***

# The Obstacle in Our Path

In ancient times, a king had a boulder placed on a roadway. Then he hid himself and watched to see if anyone would remove the huge rock. Some of the king's wealthiest merchants and courtiers came by and simply walked around it. Many loudly blamed the king for not keeping the roads clear, but none did anything about getting the big stone out of the way.

Then a peasant came along carrying a load of vegetables. On approaching the boulder, the peasant laid down his burden and tried to move the stone to the side of the road. After much pushing and straining, he finally succeeded. As the peasant picked up his load of vegetables, he noticed a purse lying in the road where the boulder had been.

The purse contained many gold coins and a note from the king indicating that the gold was for the person who removed the boulder from the roadway.

*Life presents many obstacles. My attitude towards the obstacle will determine my response. A positive*

*attitude opens doorways and creates possibilities. I still need to make effort to move in a positive direction. With the consistent practice of a positive attitude, and doing the 'work' required, life offers me rewards.*

***Every obstacle presents an opportunity to improve one's condition.***

# The Story of Two Wolves

An old Cherokee Indian chief was teaching his grandson about life. He said, "A fight is going on inside me," he told the young boy, "A fight between two wolves.

The Dark one is evil - he is anger, envy, sorrow, regret, greed, arrogance, self-pity, guilt, resentment, inferiority, lies, false pride, superiority, and ego." He continued, "The Light Wolf is good - he is joy, peace, love, hope, serenity, humility, kindness, benevolence, empathy, generosity, truth, compassion, and faith. The same fight is going on inside you grandson…and inside of every other person on the face of this earth."

The grandson ponders this for a moment and then asked, "Grandfather, which wolf will win?"

The old Cherokee smiled and simply said, "The one you feed."

*The story continues...*

However, it doesn't end there. In the Cherokee world, there's another version of the story.

The old Cherokee simply replied, "If you feed them right, they both win. You see, if I ignore the Dark wolf, it will be hiding around every corner waiting for me to become distracted or weak and jump to get the attention he craves. But if I honour and acknowledge the existence of the dark wolf, it will go to sleep."

---

*We grow what we focus on ~ whether it be positive or negative. When we resist - an idea, a person, or a system - the object of our resistance is strengthened by feeding it with our energy and attention. For sustainable positive change, I need to feed a positive vision. I have a choice ~ to feed a negative story or feed my freedom. With love and attention, I can create a feeling and image of the world I would like to see. And I can feed a positive vision of the me I would like to be. When I feed this vision daily with the energy of my attention, it will grow.*

---

***Where my attention goes,***
***my energy flows and life grows.***

# The Boat

A monk decided to meditate alone, away from his monastery. He took a boat out into the middle of the lake, closed his eyes and began to meditate.

After a few hours of unperturbed silence, he suddenly felt the bow of another boat hitting his. With his eyes still closed, he felt his anger rising and, when he opened his eyes, he was ready to shout at the boatman who dared to disturb his meditation.

But when he opened his eyes, he saw that it was an empty boat, not tied up, floating in the middle of the lake.

At that moment, the monk understood that anger was within him; it simply needed to hit an external object to be provoked.

After that, whenever he met someone who irritated or provoked his anger, he remembered; the other person is just an empty boat. Anger is inside me. *Thich Nhat Hanh*

*Knowing the difference between what IS me and what is WITHIN me is the first step to returning to peace. When I understand that I am a being of peace, I begin to make peace with myself. I recognize the energies that are not me but have taken up residence within my consciousness - anger, jealousy, greed, fear. Connected to my inner peace, I no longer seek fights, arguments, or battles of any kind. I may still stand up for something, but I will do it quietly, peacefully with no anger inside. Over time, the practice of returning to my peace dissolves anger. Discovering and expanding the peace inside me frees me from enemies outside.*

***No anger inside means no enemy outside.***

# Lessons from Ants

If you collect 100 black ants, and 100 fire ants and put them in a glass jar nothing will happen.

But if you take the jar, shake it violently and leave it on the table, the ants will start killing each other.

Red believes that black is the enemy, while black believes red is the enemy.

The real enemy is the one who shook the jar.

The same is true in society, men versus women, black versus white, faith versus science, young versus old, etc.

Before we fight each other, we must first ask ourselves: Who shook the jar? *David Attenborough*

*Shaken by difficult times, human beings turn on each other. The habit of blame creates a cycle of violence that returns to me at some point. Frustration or anger is a product of non-acceptance. There are so many things in this world that do not go as I would wish. I*

*need tolerance power to save myself from the constant inner pressure of anger and frustration. Blame intensifies intolerance. To tolerate is to accept that something is happening other than the way I would like. When I accept, I conserve my energy and create space to discover other ways to navigate in the situation. Harmony is a result of tolerance power.*

***The aim of spiritual practice is to remain calm and loving inside as the world shakes around you.***

# The Fisherman

The rich industrialist was horrified to see the fisherman lying beside his boat, smoking a pipe.

"Why aren't you out fishing," asked the industrialist?

"Because I have caught enough fish for the day." Said the fisherman.

"Why don't you catch some more?"

"What would I do with them?"

"You could earn more money. Then you could have a motor fitted to your boat to go out to deeper waters and catch more fish. Then you would have enough money to buy nylon nets. These would bring you more fish and more money. Soon you would have enough money to own two boats… maybe even a fleet of boats. Then you would be a rich man like me."

"Ah," said the fisherman. "Then what would I do?"

"Then you could sit back and enjoy life," said the industrialist, incredulous that this simple fisherman did not seem motivated to do more.

"What do you think I'm doing right now?" replied the fisherman, a smile on his face.

*Adapted from Timeless Simplicity by John Lane*

---

*The state of the world is a direct expression of humanity's state of consciousness. When human beings move faster, time speeds up. When our consumption increases, we deplete more of our planet's resources. When I am aware of the direct relationship between my own consciousness and the state of the world, I see the importance of small personal efforts to stay simple, honest and optimistic. When I uplift my consciousness I bring simplicity, generosity, peace and humility to the world.*

---

***True contentment comes from simplicity.***

# Giving

Many years ago, when I worked as a volunteer at Stanford Hospital, I got to know a little girl named Liz who was suffering from a rare and serious disease. Her only chance of recovery appeared to be a blood transfusion from her 5-year-old brother, who had miraculously survived the same disease and had developed the antibodies needed to combat the illness.

The doctor explained the situation to her little brother and asked the boy if he would be willing to give his blood to his sister.

I saw him hesitate for only a moment before taking a deep breath and saying, "Yes, I'll do it if it will save Liz."

As the transfusion progressed, he lay in bed next to his sister and smiled, as we all did, seeing the color returning to her cheeks. Then his face grew pale, and his smile faded. He looked up at the doctor and asked with a trembling voice, "Will I start to die right away?"

It took some time speaking with the little boy until I realized that he had misunderstood the doctor; he thought he was going to have to give all his blood.

*The energy of the soul is pure love. This energy is naturally expressed as generosity. We are generous by nature. We are at our best when we give of ourselves and use our time, energy, and thoughts to generate benefit for others. Generosity opens the heart and invites generosity in return. Self-less love is protected by its pure intention.*

***Pure intention is an expression of love, the true nature of the soul.***

# Dogs

There is a story about two dogs.

At separate times they enter the same room.

One comes out wagging its tail and the other comes out growling.

A woman watching this, went into the room to see what could possibly make one dog so happy and the other so mad. To her surprise she saw a room filled with mirrors.

The happy dog saw a thousand happy dogs looking back at him, while the angry dog saw only angry ones growling back at him.

*My outer world reflects my inner world. What I see around me is a mirror. My beliefs guide my actions and create my world. Beneath my beliefs lie the eternal virtues and positive qualities of the soul. When I access my virtues, I can bring my best to the world. Then my world becomes a reflection of my inner beauty.*

***When we express our best, the world reflects it back to us.***

# The Stone Cutter

Once upon a time there lived a stonecutter, who went every day to a great rock in the side of a big mountain and cut out slabs for gravestones or for houses. He understood very well the kinds of stones wanted for the different purposes, and as he was a careful work man, he had plenty of customers.

For a long time, he was quite happy and contented, and asked for nothing better than what he had. Now in the mountain dwelt a spirit which now and then appeared to men and helped them in many ways to become rich and prosperous. The stonecutter, however, had never seen this spirit, and only shook his head, with an unbelieving air, when anyone spoke of it. But a time came when he learned to change his opinion.

One day the stonecutter carried a gravestone to the house of a rich man, and saw there all sorts of beautiful things, of which he had never even dreamed. Suddenly his daily work seemed to grow harder and heavier, and he said to himself: 'Oh, if only I were a rich man, and could sleep in a bed with silken curtains and golden tassels, how happy I should be!'

And a voice answered him: 'Your wish is heard; a rich man you shall be!'

At the sound of the voice the stonecutter looked round but could see nobody. He thought it was all his fancy, and picked up his tools and went home, for he did not feel inclined to do any more work that day. But when he reached the little house where he lived, he stood still with amazement, for instead of his wooden hut was a stately palace filled with splendid furniture, and most splendid of all was the bed, in every respect like the one he had envied. He was nearly beside himself with joy, and in his new life the old one was soon forgotten.

It was now the beginning of summer, and each day the sun blazed more fiercely. One morning the heat was so great that the stonecutter could scarcely breathe, and he determined he would stay at home till the evening. He was rather dull, for he had never learned how to amuse himself, and was peeping through the closed blinds to see what was going on in the street, when a little carriage passed by, drawn by servants dressed in blue and silver. In the carriage sat a prince, and over his head a golden umbrella was held, to protect him from the sun's rays.

'Oh, if I were only a prince!' said the stonecutter to himself, as the carriage vanished round the corner.

'Oh, if I were only a prince, and could go in such a carriage and have a golden umbrella held over me, how happy I should be!' And the voice of the mountain spirit answered: 'Your wish is heard; a prince you shall be.' And a prince he was. Before his carriage rode one company of men and another behind it; servants dressed in scarlet and gold bore him along, the coveted umbrella was held over his head, everything his heart could desire was his. But yet it was not enough. He still looked round for something more to wish for. When he saw that in spite of the water he poured on his grass, the rays of the sun scorched it, and that in spite of the umbrella held over his head each day his face grew browner and browner, he cried in his anger: 'The sun is mightier than I; oh, if I were only the sun!'

The mountain spirit answered: 'Your wish is heard; the sun you shall be, and the sun he was, and felt himself proud in his power. He shot his beams above and below, on earth and in heaven; he burnt up the grass in the fields and scorched the faces of princes as well as of poorer folk. But in a short time, he began to grow tired of his might, for there seemed nothing left for him to do. Discontent once more filled his soul, and when a cloud covered his face, and hid the earth from him, he cried in his anger: 'Does the cloud hold captive my rays, and is it mightier than I? Oh, that I was a cloud, and mightier than any!'

The mountain spirit answered: 'Your wish is heard; a cloud you shall be!'

And a cloud he was and lay between the sun and the earth. He caught the sun's beams and held them, and to his joy the earth grew green again and flowers blossomed. But that was not enough for him, and for days and weeks he poured forth rain till the rivers overflowed their banks, and the crops of rice stood in water. Towns and villages were destroyed by the power of the rain, only the great rock on the mountain side remained unmoved. The cloud was amazed at the sight, and cried in wonder: 'Is the rock, then, mightier than I? Oh, if I were only the rock!'

Again, the mountain spirit answered: 'Your wish is heard; the rock you shall be!

And the rock he was and gloried in his power. Proudly he stood, and neither the heat of the sun nor the force of the rain could move him. 'This is better than all!' he said to himself. But one day he heard a strange noise at his feet, and when he looked down to see what it could be, he saw a stonecutter driving tools into his surface. Even while he looked a trembling feeling ran all through him, and a great block broke off and fell upon the ground. Then he cried in his wrath: 'Is a mere child of earth mightier than a rock? Oh, if I were only a man!' The mountain spirit answered: 'Your wish is heard. A man once more you shall be!'

And a man he was, and in the sweat of his brow he toiled again at his trade of stone cutting. His bed was hard and his food scanty, but he had learned to be satisfied with it, and did not long to be something or somebody else. As he never asked for things he had not got, or desired to be greater and mightier than other people, he was happy at last, and heard the voice of the mountain spirit no longer. *From the Crimson Fairy Book, Edited by Andrew Lang*

*Comparison creates discontent.*
*When I compare myself to another, I invalidate the unique role I play in life's drama. Each of us has a unique part to play. It takes courage to accept myself and my unique role. Happiness and contentment are a result of self-acceptance.*

***The gift of each one's life is a unique part to be played with dignity.***

*Stories are the communal currency of humanity.*

# A Bowl of Stock

An elderly lady visited a self-service restaurant. She took a bowl and asked the waiter to fill it with stock. She then sat down at one of the tables. She had barely sat down when she realized she had forgotten her bread. So, she stood up went and got her bread then returned and sat down.

Surprise! Before the bowl of stock, she found a man calmly eating.

That is the last straw thought the lady, but I am not going to let myself be robbed of my soup.

She sat down beside the man divided the bread in pieces, put them into the bowl in front of the man, and put her own spoon into the bowl.

The man obligingly smiled.

Each one had a spoonful until they finished the soup. All in silence. Once the soup was finished the man stood up, approached the bar and later returned with a large dish of spaghetti, and two forks. They both ate from the same dish in silence, taking turns.

At the end of the meal, the man got up and left.

"See you," said the lady as he left.

"See you," answered the man, with a smile in his eyes. He seemed satisfied for having done a good action, and he went out the door.

The lady followed him with her eyes. She reached back with her hand for her purse which she'd left on the back of her chair. But, to her astonishment the bag had disappeared.

That man! She thought and she was about to call out "stop that thief", when her eyes caught sight of her purse hanging two tables behind where she sat. She realized immediately what had happened.

It was not the man who had eaten her soup. It was she who had sat at the wrong table – and she, had eaten at the expense of the kind gentleman.

*From the collection of stories by the Colectivo No violencia y Education.*

*Righteousness distorts understanding. Righteousness is the feeling that I am right, and, by implication, the other is wrong. When we lose connection with each other as a human family, we create the 'other' and a sense of righteousness enters our consciousness. To meet righteousness with an attitude of righteousness divides us even further and justifies violence and war.*

**_Humility is the best response to righteousness._**

*We write the stories of our lives*
*with the pen of our actions.*

# The Striving Violet

There was a beautiful and fragrant violet who lived placidly amongst her friends and swayed happily amidst the other flowers in a solitary garden. One morning, as her crown was embellished with beads of dew, she lifted her head and looked about; she saw a tall and handsome rose standing straight and reaching high into space, like a burning torch upon an emerald lamp.

The violet opened her blue lips and said, "I would like to be as fortunate as the rose, but nature has fashioned me to be short … I live very close to the earth, and I cannot raise my head toward the blue sky, or turn my face to the sun, as the roses do."

And the rose heard her neighbour's word; she laughed and commented, "How strange is your talk! You are fortunate, and yet you cannot understand your fortune. Nature has bestowed upon you fragrance and beauty which she did not grant to any other. Cast aside your thoughts and be contented with who you are."

The violet answered, "You are consoling me because you have what I aspire to be."

And Nature heard the conversation of the violet and the rose; she approached and said, "What has happened to you, my daughter violet? You have been humble and sweet in all your deeds and words. Have you not always been satisfied with who you are?"

The violet answered her, saying. "Oh great and merciful mother, full of love, I beg you with all my heart and soul, to grant my request and allow me to be a rose for one day."

And Nature responded, "You know not what you are seeking; You are unaware of the concealed disaster behind your determination. If you were a rose, you could be sorry, and regret would avail you but naught."

The violet insisted, "Change me into a tall rose, for I wish to lift my head high with pride; and regardless of my fate, it will be my own doing."

Nature yielded, saying, "Oh violet, I will grant your request. But if calamity befalls you, your complaint must be to yourself."

And Nature stretched forth her mysterious and magic fingers and touched the roots of the violet, who immediately turned into a tall rose, rising above all flowers in the garden.

That evening, the sky become thick with black clouds, and the raging elements disturbed the silence of existence with thunder, and commenced to attack the garden, sending forth a great rain and strong winds.

The tempest tore the branches and uprooted the plants and broke the stems of the tall flowers, sparing only the little ones who grew close to the friendly earth. The solitary garden suffered greatly from the belligerent skies, and when the storm calmed and the sky cleared, all the flowers were laid waste and none of them had escaped the wrath of Nature except the clan of small violets, hiding by the wall of the garden.

Having lifted her head and viewed the tragedy of the flowers and trees, one of the violet maidens smiled happily and called to her companions, saying, "See what the tempest had done to the tall flowers!"

The queen of the violets lifted her head and called to her family, saying, "Look, my daughters, and meditate upon that which resolve has done to the violet who became a tall rose for one hour. Let the memory of this scene be a reminder of your good fortune."

And the dying rose moved and gathered the remnants of her strength, and quietly said, "I have never feared the tempest. Nature, who is the great object of our deeper dreams, granted my request and changed me into a rose with her magic fingers."

Then the rose became silent for a moment, and in a weakening voice, mingled with gratification and achievement, she said, "I have lived one hour as a tall rose; I have existed for a time like a queen; I have looked at the Universe from behind the eyes of the rose; I have heard the whisper of the firmament through the ears of the rose petals."

Having thus spoken, she lowered her head, and with a choking voice she gasped. "I shall die now, for my soul has attained its goal."

*Adapted from Kahlil Gibran*

*Life has a way of planting me in situations that are beneficial for my growth. Some situations prune me back where I am expanding in a way that disperses my life energy. Other situations nourish me deeply, enabling me to express the colour of my inner beauty.*

*When I step beyond my perceived capacity, I discover my potential. When I do something new, especially when frightening or slightly beyond my comfort zone,*

*I stretch my capacity and my perception of what is possible for me.*

***To stretch oneself is to meet one's potential.***

# The Emperor and the Flower Seeds

Long ago there lived an Emperor who loved flowers and tended his garden every day. The flowers, bushes, and trees all thrived magically. The emperor was old and knew he needed to find a successor. He decided the flowers would help him choose.

The next day he issued a proclamation to all people of the land, inviting them to the palace. There was great excitement. A young girl named Serena had always wanted to see the palace, so she decided to go. She was amazed by the splendor. Soon the emperor appeared. He walked around greeting each person and gave each one an item from a small box he carried. When he came to Serena, she saw it was a flower seed. She became the happiest of all.

The emperor announced that the person who brought back the most beautiful flower in a year's time would succeed him to the throne. Serena was very excited, and she carried the seed home carefully.

Serena placed the seed in a lovely pot with the best soil. Each day she tended it and gave it water when needed. Days passed, and nothing grew. Months passed and still nothing grew in the pot. Finally, at the year's end, it was time to return to the palace. Serena was heartbroken but felt she must keep her promise to return to show the emperor. She returned with the empty pot in her hand, noting that the others appeared with lovely flowers of every shape and size.

The emperor examined all the flowers and finally came to Serena. He asked her "Why did you bring an empty pot?" She could barely look at him. "Your Majesty I took great care to use the best soil and watered it well. Then I tried a new pot with even richer soil, but the seed didn't sprout. I did my best." The emperor smiled and took her by the hand. She wondered if she was in some type of trouble.

The emperor took her to the front of the great hall and exclaimed, "I have found my successor. The person worthy of ruling after me. The seeds I gave everyone last year had all been roasted. It wouldn't have been possible for them to grow. I don't know where your beautiful flowers have come from. Serena, I admire your great courage and honesty to appear before me with the truth. I reward you with my entire kingdom. You will be the next Empress."

*The most powerful form of honesty is to be honest with myself. This requires courage, determination and love. Courage gives me the strength to look in the places I avoid, determination keeps me from looking away and love softens my vision of myself. It is desire and ego that blind me to truth. A pure heart will see past ego and have the courage to act with honesty.*

***Honesty always wins in the end.***

# Jewels Under the Saddle

A merchant on a casual jaunt through a market came across a fine specimen of a camel for sale. The merchant and the camel seller, both skilled negotiators, struck a hard bargain. The camel seller was pleased to do this deal and he extracted what he felt was a very good price, so he parted with his camel.

Meanwhile the merchant trusted that he had struck a fantastic bargain, walked home with the latest addition to his large livestock. On arriving home, the merchant called to his servant to come and help him take off the camel saddle since the unwieldy heavily padded saddle was too difficult for the servant to manage on his own.

Hidden under the saddle the servant found a small velvet pouch.

"Master, you bought a camel but see what came free along with it."

The merchant was astonished as he looked at the jewels in his servant's palm. They were of extraordinary quality, sparkling and twinkling in the sunlight.

"I bought the camel," he said, "not the jewels. I must return them to the camel seller immediately."

The servant was against his master, thinking he was a foolish man, he said, "no one will know."

But the master headed right back to the market and handed the velvet pouch back to the camel seller. The camel seller was incredibly happy.

"I had forgotten that I hid these jewels in the saddle for safekeeping. Here choose one of the jewels for yourself as a reward."

The merchant refused, but the camel seller insisted.

Finally, the merchant said, "When I decided to bring the pouch back to you, I already took two of the most precious jewels and kept them for myself."

At this confession, the camel seller was a bit flabbergasted, and quickly emptied the pouch to count the jewels. However, he was confused, "All my jewels are here, what two did you keep?"

"The two most precious," said the merchant, "my integrity and my self-respect."

*My character is illuminated by the coherence that exists between what I say and what I do, consistently, day in and day out. To express my highest character, I must check my intentions regularly and ensure that my actions are consistent with my highest intentions. This self-alignment heightens my accuracy and integrity. This is known as making spiritual effort. True integrity is expressed when we do the right thing, even when no one is looking. My conscience is clean and my heart happy when I act with integrity.*

***Integrity is the greatest jewel of the soul.***

# Nigerian Story of Happiness

When Nigerian billionaire Femi Otedola was asked by a journalist, "Sir can you remember what made you happiest in this life?"

Femi said: "I have gone through four stages of happiness in life and finally I understood the meaning of true happiness."

The first stage was to accumulate wealth and means. But at this stage I did not get the happiness I wanted.

Then came the second stage of collecting valuables and items. But I realized that the effect of this thing is also temporary, and the luster of valuable things does not last long.

Then came the third stage of getting big projects. That was when I was holding 95% of diesel supply in Nigeria and Africa. I was also the largest vessel owner in Africa and Asia. But even here I did not get the happiness I had imagined.

The fourth stage was the time a friend of mine asked me to buy a wheelchair for some disabled children. Just about 200 kids.

At the friend's request, I immediately bought the wheelchairs. But the friend insisted that I go with him and hand over the wheelchairs to the children. I got ready and went with him.

There I gave these wheelchairs to these children with my own hands. I saw the strange glow of happiness on the faces of these children. I saw them all sitting on the wheelchairs, moving around and having fun.

It was as if they had arrived at a picnic spot where they are sharing a jackpot winning.

I felt real joy inside me. When I decided to leave one of the kids grabbed my legs. I tried to free my legs gently, but the child stared at my face and held my legs tightly.

I bent down and asked the child: "Do you need something else?"

The answer this child gave me not only made me happy but also changed my attitude to life completely.

This child said: "I want to remember your face so that when I meet you in heaven, I will be able to recognize you and thank you once again."

*and a society. Happiness is the basis of a healthy economy and a healthy person. When I am happy, I feel generous, and I contribute more. When I am unhappy, I withdraw or take. Happiness is generative. It is experienced as an abundance of inner joy. We are happiest when we are giving. Giving to others is the most powerful source of happiness.*

***The greatest happiness is to make others happy.***

# Ice Cream

In the days when an ice cream sundae cost much less, a 10-year-old boy entered a hotel coffee shop and sat at a table. A waitress put a glass of water in front of him.

"How much is an ice cream sundae?"

"Fifty cents," replied the waitress. The little boy pulled his hand out of his pocket and studied a number of coins in it. "How much is a dish of plain ice cream?" he inquired.

Some people were now waiting for a table and the waitress was a bit impatient.

"Thirty-five cents," she said brusquely.

The little boy again counted the coins.

"I'll have the plain ice cream," he said.

The waitress brought the ice cream, put the bill on the table and walked away. The boy finished the ice cream, paid the cashier, and departed.

When the waitress came back, she began wiping down the table and then swallowed hard at what she saw. There, placed neatly beside the empty dish, were two nickels and five pennies - her tip.

*True self-respect is an attitude of inner dignity. It means being loyal to the royal within me. Self-respect shapes what I do and how I do it. With careful consideration, I bring quality and virtue into each action. Then my actions are respectful towards others and my self-respect grows.*

***Respect for others is an expression of self-respect.***

# The Mirror

Once upon a time, there was a village far away from the city, and city ways. Few strangers ever came to visit. One day, a young man decided to walk to the nearest city. Nobody from the village had ever been there before, and everyone was excited that he was going on such an adventure. The young man kissed his wife goodbye before he set out on his journey.

She said to him, "Bring something back to show that you were thinking of me when you were away."

The young man said he would, and he set out on the long, long journey to the city. After a long, long walk the young man arrived at the city. He walked through streets full of people that he didn't know. They were selling all sorts of things. He didn't even know what many of the things were. He went past a shop that was selling shiny pictures. They were mirrors, but he had never seen a mirror before, so he didn't know how they worked.

He looked into the mirror and said, "That's a picture of my father as a young man. I'll bring this home to my wife, so she'll know I was thinking of her." The young man bought the mirror and walked the long, long way home to his village.

When he got home, he told his wife he had a present for her. "Let me see," she cried and took the mirror from her husband. "I thought you said it was a picture of your father," she said quite upset. "Instead, you have brought a picture of a selfish and sulking young lady."

The young man protested and tried to get the mirror back, but she wouldn't let him have it. They began to argue, and yell and quarrel until they grew so loud the neighbours came to see what the problem was.

The wife's sister looked in the mirror and said: "It is clear to me that this is a portrait of a goddess, someone accustomed to making others do her will. This picture is meant to teach my sister to obey her proud and foolish husband. I predicted something like this!"

Next the young man's uncle grabbed the mirror. "Indeed," he said "the portrait is of a face very much like your father's, young man. But firmer and more strong willed. It is a face that will bring order to a family."

Then a neighbour snatched away the mirror and looked into it. "Hah!" She said, "It's a trick! I see a portrait of one who is sly and cunning – someone pretending to be friendly but is secretly full of evil."

Everyone began to argue, and yell, and quarrel, then the wise old woman of the village showed up. She picked up the mirror and looked long and thoughtfully into it.

"This is indeed a marvel," she said. "The picture changes from moment to moment. See how it flashes? Now it gives a kind old face, one that can bring an end to quarrels. Why don't you hang this light-catcher from the rafters of the house? It can catch the spirit of heaven and shine back good luck to all of us."

And so, the first mirror of the village hung from the rafters of the young couple's house and brought peace and happiness to everyone, perhaps because that was what they expected.

*"Attitude creates atmosphere." Dadi Janki*

*Attitude is everything. It creates the atmosphere we live in. The awareness I hold in my mind, creates an attitude. This attitude is then expressed through my vibrations and influences the way I look at the world as well as my actions. I can feel the atmosphere of a place. When it is lovely, I wish to spend time there. The atmosphere is created by attitude.*

**Vision creates our world.**

# Love Is Never Blind

The passengers on the bus watched sympathetically as the attractive young woman with the white cane made her way carefully up the steps. She paid the driver and, using her hands to feel the location of the seats, walked down the aisle and found the seat he'd told her was empty. Then she settled in, placed her briefcase on her lap and rested her cane against her leg.

It had been a year since Susan, thirty-four, became blind. Due to a medical misdiagnosis, she had been rendered sightless, and she was suddenly thrown into a world of darkness, anger, frustration, and self-pity.

Once a fiercely independent woman, Susan now felt condemned by this terrible twist of fate to become a powerless, helpless burden on everyone around her. "How could this have happened to me?" she would plead, her heart knotted with anger. But no matter how much she cried or ranted or prayed, she knew the painful truth - her sight was never going to return.

A cloud of depression hung over Susan's once optimistic spirit. Just getting through each day was an exercise in frustration and exhaustion. And all she had to cling to was her husband, Mark. Mark was an Air Force officer and he loved Susan with all of his heart. When she first lost her sight, he watched her sink into despair and was determined to help his wife gain the strength and confidence she needed to become independent again. Mark's military background had trained him well to deal with sensitive situations, and yet he knew this was the most difficult battle he would ever face.

Finally, Susan felt ready to return to her job, but how would she get there? She used to take the bus but was now too frightened to get around the city by herself. Mark volunteered to drive her to work each day, even though they worked at opposite ends of the city. At first, this comforted Susan and fulfilled Mark's need to protect his sightless wife who was so insecure about performing the slightest task.

Soon, however Mark realized that this arrangement wasn't working - it was hectic, and costly. Susan is going to have to start taking the bus again, he admitted to himself. But just the thought of mentioning it to her made him cringe. She was still so fragile, so angry. How would she react?

Just as Mark predicted, Susan was horrified at the idea of taking the bus again. "I'm blind!" she responded bitterly. "How am I supposed to know where I'm going? I feel like you're abandoning me." Mark's heart broke to hear these words, but he knew what had to be done. He promised Susan that each morning and evening he would ride the bus with her, for as long as it took, until she got the hang of it.

And that is exactly what happened. For two solid weeks, Mark, military uniform and all, accompanied Susan to and from work each day. He taught her how to rely on her other senses, specifically her hearing, to determine where she was and how to adapt to her new environment. He helped her befriend the bus drivers who could watch out for her and save her a seat. He made her laugh, even on those not-so-good days when she would trip exiting the bus or drop her briefcase. Each morning they made the journey together, and Mark would take a cab back to his office.

Although this routine was even more costly and exhausting than the previous one, Mark knew it was only a matter of time before Susan would be able to ride the bus on her own. He believed in her, in the Susan he used to know before she'd lost her sight, who wasn't afraid of any challenge and who would never, ever quit. Finally, Susan decided that she was ready to try the trip on her own.

Monday morning arrived, and before she left she threw her arms around Mark, her temporary bus riding companion, her husband and her best friend. Her eyes filled with tears of gratitude for his loyalty, his patience, his love. She said good-bye, and for the first time, they went their separate ways.

Monday, Tuesday, Wednesday, Thursday ... Each day on her own went perfectly, and Susan had never felt better. She was doing it! She was going to work all by herself! On Friday morning, Susan took the bus to work as usual. As she was paying for her fare to exit the bus, the driver said, "Boy, I sure envy you."

Susan wasn't sure if the driver was speaking to her or not. After all, who on earth would ever envy a blind woman who had struggled just to find the courage to live for the past year?

Curious, she asked the driver, "Why do you say that you envy me?"

The driver responded, "It must feel so good to be taken care of and protected like you are." Susan had no idea what the driver was talking about, and asked again, "What do you mean?"

The driver answered, "You know, every morning for the past week, a fine-looking gentleman in a military uniform has been standing across the corner watching you when you get off the bus. He makes sure you cross the street safely and he watches you until you enter your office building. Then he blows you a kiss, gives you a little salute and walks away. You are one lucky lady."

*We live with the illusion of independence in a world of growing dependency. We depend on people we do not know to produce the food and materials we use on a daily basis. We cannot take care of our basic needs without many other people, even to get the simplest thing to the house (a morning cup of tea or coffee.) This creates an uncomfortable paradox called 'helpless independence'. Despite my belief that I am independent, I am increasingly dependent. When I recognize my inter-dependence, I feel more connected to my global family, and I fully appreciate the subtle threads of connection and inter-dependence that make living possible.*

***Love protects everyone.***

# Best Classroom Lesson

One day, a teacher asked her students to list the names of the other students in the room on two sheets of paper, leaving a space between each name.

Then she told them to think of the nicest thing they could say about each of their classmates and write it down. It took the remainder of the class period to finish their assignment, and as the students left the room, each one handed in the papers.

That Saturday, the teacher wrote down the name of each student on a separate sheet of paper and listed what everyone else had said about that individual.

On Monday she gave each student his or her list.

Before long, the entire class was smiling. "Really?" she heard whispered comments like, "I never knew that I meant anything to anyone!" and, "I didn't know others liked me so much."

No one ever mentioned those papers in class again. The teacher never found out if they discussed them after class or with their parents, but it didn't matter. The exercise had accomplished its purpose.

The students were happy with themselves and one another. That group of students moved on.

Several years later, one of the students was killed in Vietnam and his teacher attended the funeral of that special student. She had never seen a serviceman in a military coffin before. He looked so handsome, so mature. The church was packed with his friends. One by one those who loved him took a last walk by the coffin. The teacher was the last one to bless the coffin.

As she stood there, one of the soldiers who acted as pallbearer came up to her. "Were you Mark's math teacher?" he asked. She nodded: "Yes." Then he said: "Mark talked about you a lot."

After the funeral, most of Mark's former classmates and the teacher were invited to a luncheon. Mark's mother and father were also there, wanting to speak with his teacher.

"We want to show you something," his father said, taking a wallet out of his pocket. "They found this on Mark when he was killed. We thought you might recognize it."

Opening the billfold, he carefully removed two worn pieces of notebook paper that had obviously been taped, folded, and refolded many times. The teacher knew without looking that the papers were the ones on which she had listed all the good things each of Mark's classmates had said about him.

"Thank you so much for doing that," Mark's mother said. "As you can see, Mark treasured it."

All of Mark's former classmates started to gather around. Charlie smiled rather sheepishly and said, "I still have my list. It's in the top drawer of my desk at home."

Chuck's wife said, "Chuck asked me to put his in our wedding album." "I have mine too," Marilyn said. "It's in my diary"

Then Vicki, another classmate, reached into her pocketbook, took out her wallet and showed her worn and frazzled list to the group. "I carry this with me at all times," Vicki said. Without batting an eyelash, she continued, "I think we all saved our lists."

Tears rolled down the eyes of the humble teacher.

*Generosity means more than just giving. The greatest act of generosity is to see beyond the weaknesses of another person. A generous heart will see the best in others. When I see past a weakness, I offer a mirror for someone to see their innate value.*

*This requires a generosity of spirit, a big heart. It is the greatest give we can give another human being.*

***Being a mirror for someone's goodness is a gift that keeps giving.***

# Get on the Bus

Once during a spiritual retreat in India, I learned a valuable lesson about relationships. Part of my reason for being in the retreat was to learn how to create right relationships with people. I felt I carried parents, siblings, aunties, uncles, cousins, friends, co-workers, partners, clients and many other people around with me in my mind. I spent a lot of time thinking about my relationships until they took all the space in my mind and lived there permanently! Like me, I'm sure you have a long list of personal relationships!

The idea was presented in the retreat that we could learn to love everyone, yet not be attached to them. That, to be truly free, we needed to break attachment and dependencies, yet keep the love. Why would I want to do this, I asked myself? I was learning how important it was to take care of myself so I could be caring to others. This became my key focus in the retreat. I reflected on the extent to which I was emotionally attached to people and decided I would make changes and feel lighter and less burdened in my relationships.

One day, we took a trip to a beautiful garden called Peace Park. I love gardens so I went along for the day. On the bus, I sat beside a very interesting couple from Morocco who were staying at the same campus. We struck up a conversation and enjoyed each other's company immensely on the way to the gardens.

When we arrived at the gardens, we continued to walk together in the beauty of the rose garden. At a green patch in the park, some games were being played and I decided I wanted to stay. They continued walking and we agreed to meet back at the bus to share the journey back to the campus.

The visit to the gardens passed quickly. Soon it was time to return. I walked through the garden on the way back to the bus keeping an eye out for my new friends. I did not see them and supposed I had missed them somehow in the large garden.

The bus was waiting, and people had started to board. I looked through the windows to see if they were already on the bus, but there was no sign of them. It was here we had promised to meet each other and so I decided to wait for them. As the bus filled, I was aware I might be waiting a full hour before the next bus came. Although it would be inconvenient, I had made a promise, so I decided to stay back in case my new friends arrived late.

Then one of my mentors, Francis, arrived. We greeted each other and he asked, "How come you're not on the bus?" I told him, "I'm waiting for two new friends I promised to meet here. They may be lost."

He looked at me, calm and cool and said in an authoritative voice. "Debbie, get on the bus."

As soon as he said it, I understood what was happening. To get on the bus was to honour myself. By waiting, I was binding myself to a situation over which I had no control. Francis may well have said, "Cut the strings now before you tie yourself up to more people."

The years of habitual attachment and dependencies flashed through my mind. This was a little test paper designed especially for me.

A little note in the drama. Two days later I bumped into my new friends. We had a quick reunion and they told me they had missed me at the bus because another friend had offered them a ride back in her car. End of story for them.

*Waiting can become a habit. I wait for the weekend, or for an opportunity or for someone to change. Each situation requires a unique response. Waiting is a passive response. The consciousness of being alert and*

*open makes me ever ready to respond to life accurately.*

***"Get on the bus" has become a personal mantra for not 'waiting' around for anyone or anything to bring me happiness.***

# Winter

"The winter of the world is upon us." He said, his face set firm. Only the twinkle in his eye indicated a quiet delight for life.

"What does that mean, Master?" asked his new apprentice.

"What do you think it means?" he asked, always the teacher.

"That everything is dying? Including humanity?" His voice was a whisper, afraid it was true.

"Ahhh you see, there is the mistake!" The master's voice rippled with excitement as he responded. "Seeing death as the end. Death is only a beginning."

"What?" Incredulous, the 12-year-old boy stared up at his new master, his face partly filled with fear and partly awestruck by his master's wisdom and experience.

No one had ever shown him the kindness that this old man had since he arrived to live with him only a month before. Each morning, a tiny tray of biscuits and hot tea awaited him when he opened his door at dawn to begin the day's work. He had known only beatings and fear before coming here. Now he was beginning to expect kindness.

"Winter is a time for nature to rest, to put all its energy into the roots beneath the cold ground. It is time to protect the seeds for the new season. It is a beautiful, precious time. Even if it looks dead to our eyes, there is life beneath the surface."

And the boy looked up at the master and said, "And even you?"

The great master smiled in response. "Ah my child, not me, only my body."

They lived together for years until the spirit of the master left the old man's body behind. The young apprentice was now older himself. And he left a little tray of tea and biscuits outside the door of his young apprentice every morning.

---

*"To get better at wintering, we need to address our very notion of time. We tend to imagine that our lives are linear, but they are in fact cyclical. Befriending this cyclical rhythm of our inner lives, we emerge from the*

*coldest season of the soul not only undiminished but revitalized."* Katherine May

---

**Bodies age and die,
consciousness continues.**

# Forever

"Mommy what happens when we die?"

How is it that children ask the deepest questions right before sleep?

My daughter looked up at me through sleepy eyes as I tucked her into bed for the night. She held her stuffed elephant close so she could squeeze him tight in the night.

"Well sweetheart, there are lots of different ideas about that. I'll tell you what I think."

She smiled at me as only a 5-year-old can, full of trust in the unquestionable authority of her mom.

"I think you're a little star. And you light up this body with your life energy. That's why you sparkle and are so full of energy. And when it's time to go to another place and to be with other loved ones, you leave this body behind."

Does that mean I have to leave you?" she looked distressed.

"Well yes or I leave you first. We never know when someone is ready to go. But the thing is, we can never ever lose each other."

"But how will you find me Mom? How will you know where to look if I leave?"

"I think we just know where to find each other. Because we know each other so well and because we love each other so much, our hearts find each other."

"But how will you know it's me?"

"I'll just know."

She looked at me, her long eye lashes starting to close over her big eyes, heavy with fatigue.

"But most important now is that this little star get some sleep. I love you sweetheart."

"I love you too Mom."

*The body is made from the elements of nature. It is ruled by the laws of the material world. The spirit is energy which cannot be destroyed. Considering this possibility brings reassurance and security.*

***Soul connections are eternal.***

# Two Birds

Two birds were very happy in the same tree, a willow tree. One of them rested on a branch at the highest part of the willow, the other one was down below, where one branch joined another. After a while the bird perched on the highest part of the tree said, "Oh what beautiful green leaves these are!"

The bird resting on the branch below took this statement as a provocation. He replied in a curt manner: "Are you blind? Can't you see that they are white?"

The bird on the upper branch said, "It is you who is blind, they are green!"

The other bird said: "I'll bet my tail feathers that they are white."

The bird at the top felt his temper flare and without thinking jumped down on the same branch as his adversary. They were both angry and fluffed out their feathers ready to fight. As is the custom, they looked up before they started the fight.

The bird who'd come down from above said: "How strange! Look at the leaves they are white."

He invited his friend: "Come up where I was before."

They flew to the highest branch of the willow tree and looked down at the leaves below. Then both exclaimed together, "Look at the leaves they are so green."

*"Opinion is really the lowest form of human knowledge. The highest form is empathy, for it requires us to suspend our egos and live in another's world."*
*Bill Bullard*

*Empathy, as the highest knowledge, prepares me to live well. It helps me understand how the world works and also how human hearts work. Understanding the human heart helps me 'feel the pulse' so I can contribute in a beneficial way. Today let me bring knowledge into practice through empathy.*

***Joining someone on their 'branch' creates understanding and empathy and dissolves conflict.***

# Butterfly

A man found a cocoon of a butterfly. One day a small opening appeared. He sat and watched the butterfly for several hours as it struggled to force its body through that little hole. Then it seemed to stop making any progress. It appeared as if it had gotten as far as it could, and it could go no further. So, the man decided to help the butterfly. He took a pair of scissors and snipped off the remaining bit of the cocoon. The butterfly then emerged easily. But it had a swollen body and small, shriveled wings.

The man continued to watch the butterfly because he expected that, at any moment, the wings would enlarge and expand to be able to support the body, which would contract in time. Neither happened! In fact, the butterfly spent the rest of its life crawling around with a swollen body and shriveled wings. It never was able to fly.

What the butterfly needed was to push against the restricting cocoon so the struggle required to get through the tiny opening would force fluid from the body of the butterfly into its wings so that it would be ready for flight once it achieved its freedom from the cocoon.

*Obstacles strengthen our wings to fly!*
*Just like the butterfly, we become stronger with each obstacle we face. Each problem offers an opportunity to strengthen something inside me, a personal quality, an attitude, or a response. Hard or challenging situations serve to strengthen my heart.*

***Beneath the noise and turmoil of the current times, is a heartbeat of humanity growing stronger and stronger.***

# The Star

Once upon a time there was a sparkling star who came to earth to shine.

She was sweet and innocent, and the world welcomed her with open arms and lots of love. She danced and played with the plants and animals, happy and free.

Over time, her light faded until it became quite dim. She did not know what to do. Finally, one day, she looked up into the sky from where she had come.

She saw the biggest Star of all, that shone like a sun. The Star gave her the gift of power, and she shone brightly again!

*Although we look to physical things to recharge the battery of the soul, only spiritual energy can empower me.*

***Light restores light.***

# The Ramayana Retold

Once upon a time there was a queen named Sita. She was married to a king named Rama. Rama was the perfect king, the perfect son, the perfect father, and the perfect husband. They lived very happily together.

Outside their kingdom lived a demon, named Ravan, who wanted to kidnap Sita. But he could not easily harm Sita because there was a line of protection drawn around her! If Sita stayed within the line, she was safe.

But Ravan found clever ways to tempt her to cross the line.

One day when Rama and Sita were having a picnic in the forest, Rama heard the call of a beautiful bird. He went to see what it was. But drew a line in the ground around Sita so she would be safe.

Ravan took his chance and transformed himself into a beggar. He stayed just far enough outside the line that he was not easily reached and asked Sita for food.

Feeling sorry for the beggar, Sita reached for food from their picnic and her toe touched the line as she reached out to give it to the beggar.

Instantly the beggar transformed into the 10-headed demon Ravan and kidnapped her, taking her to the Cottage of Sorrow where she was trapped for 14 years.

Ravan was not just an ordinary monster, he had 10 heads. Sita became a slave to the 10 heads that needed constant feeding. Each time a head was fed, it grew bigger and wanted more. Sita was busy all the time.

Her beloved Rama tried everything to free her. Then he asked God for help. And God suggested he send a message to Sita. So, Rama sent a message which said, "I can free you, but there is one condition. The condition is from God."

Now God is a loving Being, who has no selfish motives or desires, and only wants what is best for each child. What could be the condition?

Sita read the note and discovered the condition was, "You must decide if you truly want to become free."

This was the Godly condition.

The choice was obvious. One would think it would be easy to choose between being the Queen to Rama or a slave to Ravan.

But…

But it was not an easy decision. Why?

Because Ravan had a clever assistant called Maya.

Over the days and weeks imprisoned, Maya had befriended Sita. Every time Sita made the decision to be free, Maya gave her advice.

One time Maya said "Tell him to come later; you are tired today after all your hard work." And Sita waited.

Another time Maya said, "It is difficult, so many people have tried and failed, he will not get through, why do you want to bother?"

And Sita had doubt and waited.

Another time Maya said, "You are weak, you crossed the line, and you are responsible for this. Why should you put Rama at risk for your mistake?"

And Sita felt guilty and waited.

Another time Maya gave Sita something to distract her, she said, "Okay stop worrying about this situation, let's have a snack and take a break from this worry."

And Sita waited.

Maya was a master of persuasion.

She said things like, "It's a gradual process, it might not work straight away, it may take a few years."

And each time Sita waited.

Until one day, when Sita was washing a big shiny stainless-steel bowl. Her hands were broken and chapped. Her heart was dispirited, and she thought she would never get out of this place.

Then she saw her face reflected in the bowl.

A funny thing happened.

Why had she never noticed this before? She saw a tiny star shining in the centre of her forehead in the exact place she used to wear a sparkling diamond as a sign of her royalty.

She looked into her own eyes for the first time in weeks and months.

And she began to remember.

She remembered who she was. "I am a Queen!" she almost cried with joy at the realization. "I am not a slave!"

"Yes Rama, YES!!! I WANT TO BE FREE!!!"

And Rama's army brought her home to the kingdom. And the people in the kingdom turned on all the lights to celebrate Sita's return. Today we call this celebration Diwali.

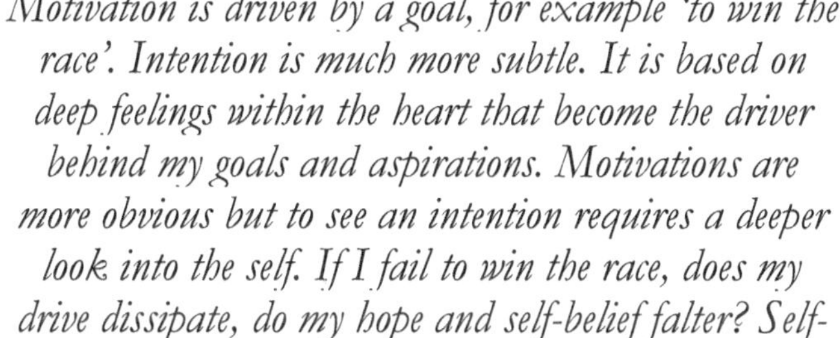

*Motivation is driven by a goal, for example 'to win the race'. Intention is much more subtle. It is based on deep feelings within the heart that become the driver behind my goals and aspirations. Motivations are more obvious but to see an intention requires a deeper look into the self. If I fail to win the race, does my drive dissipate, do my hope and self-belief falter? Self-respect is at the root of pure intention. Understanding who I am gives me the strength and resilience to carry on.*

***Remembering who I am sets me free. God's help comes when I am ready to accept it.***

# Unseen Blessings

A man whispered, "Creator speak to me" and a meadowlark sang. But the man did not hear.

So, the man yelled, "Universe, speak to me" and the thunder rolled across the sky, but the man did not listen.

The man looked around and said, "Let me see you." And a star shined brightly. But the man did not see.

And, the man shouted, "Divine Spirit, show me a miracle." And, a life was born, but the man did not notice.

So, the man cried out in despair,

"Touch me and let me know you are here." Whereupon, the Great Mystery touched the man, but the man brushed the butterfly away and walked on.

*We are uplifted by the energy of blessings. When I have brought benefit to others, the energetic return is a*

*silent good wish ~ blessings ~ from their heart. This acts as powerful energy to uplift and move me forward on my own life journey. God's blessings work in the same way ~ to give me a lift, to find solutions and to receive what life is offering me. Sometimes blessings are so subtle I have to be open to see.*

**Stay open to receive blessings as they often arrive in unexpected forms.**

*What does God really do for us?*

*In every culture and religion, God is given names that suggest the role He/She has played in our lives.*

*Divine Source, Ocean of Peace, Ocean of Love, Remover of Sorrow, Bestower, Merciful One, Liberator.*

*God gives the pure energy of spiritual power to the soul.*

*Each soul is a cherished child whose journey is unique. Each will experience the return of their own actions/karma ~ positive or negative.*

*God is not there to judge.*

*God is there to support, uplift and empower.*

# Hidden Treasure

It is a little-known secret that God visits the human world when it is so dark that the human heart can no longer find the light. The Supreme Light comes to bring light, to purify the old world and restore it and all its inhabitants to their original pure state. Then God retires until the darkness comes again.

Before leaving for retirement, God called a group of Angels together to ask for their ideas of where to hide the memory of light and goodness so humans would not find it during the dark period, until it was time for God's return.

Very quickly one Angel suggested: "You could hide the memory of their light deep in the Earth."

"Good thought," replied God, always encouraging. "As we know, humans will start eagerly mining and digging deep into the earth to uncover all its treasures. They would discover My light too quickly."

"You could hide their goodness on the moon, its further away" offered a second Angel.

"Well," said God, "It would take them longer to reach the moon, but we know they have the capacity to fly and in time they will reach the moon. If they uncover the knowledge of their goodness, they would not have the necessary time to grow spiritually."

"You could hide this memory in the cats and dogs and all of nature," said a third Angel.

"You are forgetting indeed they do decide, among themselves, that I am there! Then they stop searching and growing and believe everything around them is divine, the great myth of omnipresence. Eventually, however, they will see nature degraded and will know I am not there."

Given God's knowledge of the drama plan, the Angels thought some more about the generous amount of time God wanted to give the humans to explore themselves to find their divine natures. After some thought another Angel suggested: "You could hide it deep within their own hearts, they would never think of looking there!"

"That's it!" said God, knowing this would be the perfect hiding pace.

And so it is that the memory of human goodness and God's part in recreating the light were hidden deep in the hearts of every one of God's creations. And they never thought to look there.

Until one day, when all else had failed, they looked within. They dared to risk the great journey to the very core of their being. And there, discovered their own goodness and power.

*We have developed a habit of looking outside ourselves to find what the soul needs. With wealth, adventure, relationships, and sense pleasures, we are still unable to satisfy the soul. Somewhere deep inside, we carry a memory of a beautiful time, stored as feelings and images buried in the subconscious and carried across the centuries. We remember when we are reminded, sometimes by an absence or longing so deep, we search within to find its source.*

***The greatest buried treasure is ~ myself.***

# The Diamond & the Monk

There once was a monk who meditated in silence on a mountaintop.

One day, a man came running to the top of a mountain where a monk was sitting.

He saw the monk and rushed to him yelling, "Stone, stone, where is the stone?"

The monk tried to think what this is all about but did not understand. So, he continued in his silent meditation.

The man then came to him and said "Last night I had a dream, and in the dream, God told me to go to this very mountain where I would meet a monk, sitting in a certain place, and that monk would give me a stone. And that stone would make me rich forever."

He paused, he could see the monk was serene and undisturbed by his abrupt arrival.

"So," he continued, "I got up early and came here and just as I was told in the dream you are sitting here. So where is the stone?" he demanded.

"Oh, now I know what you are talking about," said the monk. "There is a stone over there under the tree. Take it and it will make you rich."

So, the man went to the tree and sure enough there was a stone. It was not an ordinary stone. It was a diamond. Very excited to find such a valuable gem, the man took the diamond, hid it in his bag and went home as quickly as possible.

A week passed. Then the man came back up the mountain looking for the monk.

The monk was serene and peaceful.

The man was distressed as he told the monk his story.

"I am possibly the richest man in town but for this whole week I have been having panic attacks. I am worried about the diamond. I do not trust the banks. I do not trust my friends, or neighbours. I am constantly worried that someone will steal my diamond."

He looked at the monk, so calm and serene. Again, the monk was not disturbed by the man's presence.

Then the man had an idea. Perhaps he had been looking for the wrong thing. Calmly, he sat next to the monk and asked.

"Can you tell me what wealth you have that allowed you to give away such a valuable diamond?"

---

*"Greed is not written into our biology but is a mere symptom of the perception of scarcity." Charles Eisenstein*

*Abundance is a state of consciousness based on appreciation. When I know that I have everything of value within me, when I enjoy the silence of my own inner world, I do not need to search outside myself for a sense of completion. Wisdom is found in silence. Behind the words, behind the feelings, behind the thoughts lies a place of deep quiet and calm. Here is where wisdom resides ~ in the quiet core of my being. Wisdom is spiritual wealth.*

---

***Spiritual wisdom is the true wealth of the soul.***

# The Old Man and the King

King Janak was a king, well-known for his knowledge and charity. He lived in a splendid palace but wished to achieve enlightenment. He made it known that he would listen to anyone in his kingdom who could tell him about the method for receiving spiritual liberation.

All the sages and holy men from far and wide came to visit him and gave very learned discourses and scholarly lectures, but no one was able to fulfill the king's request. He was disappointed and thought of giving up the whole idea, for the scholars had given nothing of substance. Finally, the king announced that anyone else who thought that he might have the correct answer to the problem and who could satisfy his thirst for knowledge was welcome to speak.

An old man stepped forward. The king asked if he had something to contribute.

"Yes," he said, "but your majesty, I must say something about this gathering. I hope that none of you will be angered by my frankness."

The sages looked tense for they did not like this elderly sage. His body was crippled with age and the 8 deformities he had from birth. His countenance was unpleasant to behold, and he had been shunned by the other sages for years.

Some of them grinned, others were seen grinding their teeth, and gossiping amongst themselves. In contrast, the king sat calm and composed, listening attentively and patiently.

Continuing, the old sage said "Forgive me for my rudeness, your Royal Highness! Royal Sages, I respect you all for your learning and wisdom, but may I ask you why you all laughed so scornfully, when you saw me entering the courtyard? Wasn't it my ugly body with its bends and twists that made you mock me? Doesn't this then speak rather eloquently of your physical-mindedness?"

They now, all appeared to be realizing their mistake, but the expressions of scorn had not left their faces.

The ugly man continued, "Am I wrong to point out that spiritual consciousness is the means to enlightenment? Therefore, looking at the body, without seeing the soul, and hatefully scorning the person for their condition, would you call such a person a sage?"

The king looked on with interest.

"No," continued the old sage. "Such a person looks only at the outer flesh, the skin, and therefore, I would have to call him a dealer-in skin."

On hearing this, King Janak achieved enlightenment and became even more respected than the many famous sages around him.

*The external form of something is not an accurate indicator of what lies inside. When "looking good" is important, there is over-attention to the form and shape of a person, their role, position and reputation. These are unreliable indicators of the qualities of a person's character. Freeing ourselves from using external indicators of success opens us to see the subtle, spiritual clues of wisdom and ultimately enlightenment. This spiritual consciousness is the means to true liberation.*

***True liberation comes when we are spirit-conscious not body-conscious.***

# Fire in the Jungle

A gigantic fire broke out in the jungle. The animals flocked together on the other side of the lake, and they gazed at the flames. A small bird, seeing what was going on, took a drop of water in its little beak and let it drop on the flames. It returned, took another little drop of water in its little beak and let it drop on the flames. And like this it flew back and forth diligently.

The rest of the animals just watched him and said to each other.

"And does this one think he can actually do something with his little drop of water?"

At one stage they asked him "Tell us little bird, do you honestly believe you can put out the fire with your little drops of water?"

The little bird answered "I do what I must".

Just then, an angel went by, saw the little bird and produced a great rainfall.

The fire went out.

*Taken from: "Visions of a Better world", by Henny Trailes*

*We have enough smart people and good ideas to eradicate all the troubles humanity faces. Yet we lack the energy of cooperation to implement these good ideas and get traction over time. To build momentum we must have staying power so we do not get distracted by the next idea that arises. We must be willing to give up something to get something else (delayed gratification) and we must be willing to offer our support to ideas that were not ours (trust). These qualities of focus, discipline and trust are spiritual qualities. Effort for a worthy cause is never wasted. A better world is built with cooperation.*

**A drop at a time creates a lake.**

# Frederick

Once upon a time there was a family of field mice that lived in a stone wall on the edge of a meadow. It was the beginning of fall and because winter was not far off the mice began to gather corn and nuts and wheat and straw and berries. They all worked day and night all except a little mouse named Frederick.

One day when the mice were collecting yellow corn, they asked Frederick "Frederick why don't you work?"

"I do work," said Frederick "I gather sun rays for the cold dark winter days."

On a day when they were carrying nuts back to their home in the Stonewall the mice noticed that Frederick was looking out into the meadow.

"And now Frederick," they asked. "And now what are you doing?"

"I am catching their colours," answered Frederick "because winter is grey."

And once when the mice were gathering straw Frederick seemed half asleep.

"Are you dreaming Frederick?" asked the other mice but Frederick said, "Oh no I am gathering words because the winter days are long, and we'll run out of things to say."

Finally, the winter arrived and when the first snow fell the mice ran into their home in the stone wall. It was warm in their nest of straw and they felt very good knowing they had harvested so much food for the long winter.

In the beginning there was lots to eat, and the mice told each other silly stories. They were a happy family. But little by little they nibbled up most of the nuts and berries and the corn was only a memory. They were hungry. The winter was cold. Spring was still many days away and nobody felt like talking. Then they remembered what Frederick had said about the sun's rays and colours and words.

"What about your supplies Frederick? How about your harvest?" all the mice asked.

"Close your eyes," said Frederick as he climbed up on a big stone. "Now I send you the rays of the sun, do you feel their golden glow?" And as Frederick spoke of the sun, the other little mice began to feel a little warmer.

"And now the colours Frederick?" ask the mice.

"Close your eyes again," Frederick said, and he told them of bluebells red poppies yellow wheat and the green leaves of the berry bush. The little mice saw the colours as clearly as if they were painted in their minds.

"And the words Frederick?" a mouse asked.

Frederick cleared his throat waited a moment and then said, "Who scatters the snowflakes?

*Who melts the ice?*

*Who spoils the weather? Who makes it nice?*

*Who grows the four-leaf clover in June?*

*Who dims the daylight? Who likes the Moon?*

*Four little field mice who live in the sky,*

*Four little field mice like you and I.*

*One is the spring mouse who turns on the showers*

*Then comes summer who paints in the flowers*

*The fall Mouse is next with walnuts and wheat.*

*And winter is last with little cold feet.*

*Aren't we lucky the seasons are four?*

*Think of a year with one less or one more.*

When Frederick had finished, they all applauded. And they passed the dark winter cheerfully together until the spring came.

*"We have art so that we shall not die of reality."*
*Nietzsche*

*Beauty awakens something deep in the soul ~ beyond the mundane and ordinary. Art is an expression of creativity, the very lifeblood of the human spirit. Art offers a respite and a reframe of reality. Every day is an opportunity to create. The canvas is my mind, the brushes and colours are my thoughts and feelings and the picture is a vision for a better, more beautiful world. To see something in my mind or on a canvas is the start of creating a new reality.*

***To weather hard times, we need to feed the spirit as well as the stomach.***

# Living Fearlessly

While meditating late at night, a saint saw a ghost of the dreaded smallpox entering the village where she lived.

"Stop Mr. Ghost," she said. "Do not molest the town where I worship God."

"I will take only three people," the ghost replied. "In accordance with my karmic duty."

At this the saint unhappily nodded.

The following day three persons died of smallpox. The next day more people died and each day more people were overcome by the fearful disease.

Thinking that a great deception had been played on her, the saint meditated deeply and summoned the ghost. When it came the saint rebuked it and said, "Mr. Ghost you deceived me and did not speak the truth when you said you'd take only three people with your smallpox."

But the ghost replied, "By the Great Spirit I did speak the truth to you."

The saint persisted. "You said you'd only take three persons and scores have succumbed."

"I took only three." said the ghost. "The rest died of fear."

*Shri Shri Paramen Yagamunda*

*"Hope is that thing inside us that insists, despite all the evidence to the contrary, that something better awaits us if we have the courage to reach for it and to work for it and to fight for it." Barak Obama*
*Fear causes the soul to lose hope. When afraid, we perceive everything as a threat, and some give up. But with hope, we make the best choices we can to keep ourselves safe and look to the future when all will be well.*

***The human spirit thrives on hope.***

# Roots

There once was an old lady who had many, many plants. In fact, plants were her best friends. She liked plants more than she liked people. Plants were always very good to her. She could almost feel them smiling when she watered them. And it was like a burst of laughter every time they bloomed a new leaf or flower. She watched them grow from tiny saplings to big plants and trees.

But one day, she couldn't see the plants anymore as she was losing her eyesight. And her arms were growing weak, making it difficult to lift the watering can. This made her very sad.

Every day, she reached out a tender hand as she felt around the living room to find each plant. When she got close, she pointed a gentle finger outward until she felt the leaves.

"Ah, a strong, waxy leaf," she said aloud, "That must be you, dear jade plant. Hello."

When she felt the light, fluffy fairy-like leaves, she gasped in wonder, "Oh it's you my English Vine friend."

She caressed the plants and talked to them all day. And in this way, she loved them.

But one day, when her arms had grown very weak, she tried to water the plants, but couldn't reach them with the watering bucket. Even when she held it with both hands, it did not reach high enough to water the plants, even though they tried to reach out their leaves to meet the watering bucket.

The old lady took the one thing she could lift and sprayed all the leaves, hoping that would give them something to drink.

But bit by bit, the leaves began to shrivel.

Then they began to get a little crispy and when she reached out to touch them, they crumbled and broke in her hand. This made the old lady so, so sad she did not know what to do.

Then one day, the lady disappeared. She was in the hospital and the plants were left alone.

A little girl came with her mom to see her grandmother's house and gather up her granny's belongings. She saw the plants, dry and wilted and began to cry.

"Mama, mama, these are granny's special friends. And they are all dry and unhappy. We have to do something!"

And the mom helped the little girl lift the heavy watering can. She watered every plant, slowly so they would not be overwhelmed by the sudden gush of water when they were so parched.

And she waited. And waited. And waited.

It took many days and a few visits until finally the plants were happy again. They smiled at the little girl with their green, shiny leaves and the little girl knew her granny would be happy when she came home.

*The roots connecting humanity are the timeless values and virtues known to all, taught in all religious and spiritual paths. Time spent at the surface of life, taking care of the leaves of expression will not nourish the deep roots that hold us together. Watering the roots means feeding the spirit of humanity, keeping virtues and values alive in our actions, our communities and our institutions.*

***Life grows when we water the roots.***

# Stone Soup

Once upon a time there were three soldiers. They had been walking for days with no food. Eventually they came to a town. The people of the town had seen the hungry soldiers before, and they said to themselves "Soldiers are always hungry. We would like to feed them, but we have so little food. We had better hide what we have." So, the villagers hid their carrots, their cabbages, their barley, and their milk. In fact, they hid all the food in the village.

The three soldiers stopped at the first house and politely knocked on the door. "Excuse me" said the first soldier, "Have you got a little food for three hungry soldiers?" But the people of the house sadly shook their heads no. The same thing happened at the second house and the third house. All the villagers stood in the village square and sighed and tried to look as hungry as they could.

The soldiers talked among themselves, then, the first soldier called out: "Good people! We see that you too are hungry. Well then, we'll just have to make stone soup". The people stared. Stone soup? Now this would be something to know about, "First we will need a big pot," said the second soldier. "Then we will need a big fire," said the third soldier.

"And we will need buckets of water," said the first soldier. The villagers were so curious about stone soup that they got the things that the soldiers asked for. Soon there was a big pot of boiling water in the middle of the village square. "Now," said the first soldier, we need three good stones," and he picked up three stones from the village square and plopped them into the pot. "Stones like these make wonderful soup." The villagers were amazed.

After a while the soldiers tasted the soup. "Hmmm," said one of the soldiers, "it is very good, but it needs some salt and pepper."

Children raced each other to see who could bring the salt and pepper to the soldiers first. The soldiers put some salt and pepper into the pot with the water and stones. The soldiers tasted the soup again. "This is very good soup indeed," said one of the soldiers, "but it would be excellent with a few carrots. But there's no sense in asking for what we don't have."

One of the women of the village said, "I think I have a carrot or two," and she ran back to her house and came back with six carrots. The soldiers cut them up and placed them in the soup. Then they tasted the soup again.

"Oh yes, an excellent soup, but it would be truly superb if it had a little cabbage in it. But there's no sense of asking for what we don't have." One of the men of the village thought that he might have a cabbage and he returned with three cabbages he'd hidden when the soldiers arrived. The soldiers put the cabbage in the soup and tasted the soup again.

"This is a truly superb soup," said one of the soldiers, "but the last time we served the king stone soup we also added a little barley and some milk. But there's no sense in asking for what we don't have."

The villager's eyes were wide with wonder! These soldiers had served soup to the king. A soup so superb, and yet made from just a few stones. It seemed like magic. So, they all went back to their homes and came back with barley, milk, potatoes, and parsley.

At last, the soup was ready. Great tables were set in the square. Each person slowly tried the strange stone soup. It was delicious. Never had the village tasted such a soup and there was plenty for all. "We will never be hungry again", said the villagers. "Thank you so much for teaching us how to make soup from stones."

"Ahh", said the first soldier, "it's all in knowing how."

*Love creates cooperation.*
*Where there is love, people are ready to surrender their time, wealth, and cooperation. When I have pure intention to benefit others, it is felt. It opens hearts and makes others respond in a loving way This love enables all types of cooperation.*

***Cooperation feeds us all.***

# Hands

"Grandma how do you deal with pain?"

"With your hands, dear. When you do it with your mind, the pain hardens even more."

“With your hands, grandma?”

"Yes, yes. Our hands are the antennas of our Soul. When you move them by sewing, cooking, painting, touching the earth or sinking them into the earth, they send signals of caring to the deepest part of you and your Soul calms down. This way she doesn't have to send pain anymore to show it.”

"Are hands really that important?"

"Yes, my girl. Think of babies, they get to know the world thanks to their touch. When you look at the hands of older people, they reveal more about their lives than any other part of the body.

Everything that is made by hand, so it is said, is made with the heart because it really is like this, hands and heart are connected.

Think of lovers, when their hands touch, they love each other in the most sublime way."

"My hands grandma, how long since I used them like that!"

"Move them my love, start creating with them and everything in you will move.

The pain will not pass away. But it will be the best masterpiece. And it won't hurt as much anymore because you managed to embroider your Essence."
*Elena Barnabé*

*When faced with an obstacle or difficult situation and uncertain how to proceed, I delay action until I have clarity. Sometimes it is the consistent repetition of small, positive actions that will create clarity. Inertia and inactivity can feed a sense of being 'stuck'. My decision to act, with even the smallest action, serves as a catalyst for clarity. Positive momentum starts with small steps, repeated consistently over time.*

***The world will change when the love in our hearts finds practical expression through our hands.***

# Old Turtle

Once upon a time, long, long ago, when all the animals and rocks and winds and waters and trees and birds and fish and all the beings of the world could sleep and understand one another, there began an argument.

It began softly at first. Quiet as the breeze it whispered: "Peace is like the wind that is never still." Quiet as the stone that answered, "Peace is a great rock and never moves."

Gentle as the mountain that rumbled: "Peace is a snowy peak, high above the clouds." And the fish in the ocean that answered: "Peace is a swimmer, in the dark blue depths of the sea."

"No", said the star, "Peace is a twinkling and a shining far, far away."

"No" said the ant: "Peace is a sound and a smell and a feeling that is very, very close."

And the argument grew louder and louder and LOUDER, until a new voice spoke. It rumbled loudly like thunder, and it whispered softly like a butterfly sneeze. The voice came from an old turtle. Old turtle hardly ever said anything, and certainly never argued about Peace. But now, Old Turtle began to speak.

"Peace is indeed swift and free as the wind, and still and silent as a great rock," she said to the breezes and stones. "Peace is indeed deep," she said to the fish, "and much higher than high" she said to the mountains. "Peace is always close by, yet beyond the farthest twinkling light," she told the ant and the star. "Peace is gentle and powerful and above all things and within all things."

Old Turtle had never said so much before. All the beings of the world were very surprised, and they became very quiet. Old Turtle had one more thing to say: "There will soon be a new family of beings in the world," she said "and they will be strange and wonderful. They will come in many colours and shapes, with different faces and different ways of speaking. Their thoughts will soar to the stars, but their feet will walk on the earth. They will possess many powers. They will be strong, yet tender. They will be called people, and they will be a message of Peace to the world."

And the people came. But after a while, people forgot they were a message of Peace to the world. And they began to argue about who knew the best way to live together in Peace, and who did not. Often people misused their powers, and hurt one another, or even killed one another. They also hurt the earth. Until finally the forests and the rivers and the oceans and the plants and the animals and the earth itself began to die. All because the people forgot how to live together in Peace.

Then one day there came some voices, and the voices were loud as thunder and as soft as a butterfly sneeze. The voices came from the mountains who rumbled: "Sometimes I see Peace in the depths of the sea," the fish said. "Sometimes, I feel Peace as I see the sun reflected of the snow-capped mountains."

The stones said, "Sometimes I feel Peace in the wind as it blows by."

The breeze said, "Sometimes I feel Peace as I dance among the stones."

The Star said, "Sometimes Peace is a distant and twinkling light."

After a very long, lonesome, and scary time, the people began to listen and began to hear the mountains and the fish and the wind and the stones and the star and the ant, and the people began to be at Peace again.

They had Peace again with one another, and at Peace with all the beauty of the earth. Old Turtle smiled.

*The story of humanity runs back a long way. Some say it begins with a period of savagery that progresses to this modern time. Others say the civilizations came before and life has now degraded to include sorrow and suffering for all, even the affluent. What if the current chapter is a period of transformation for humanity, where material-mindedness is destroyed and we awaken to what matters most ~ love and peace?*

***Peace is the original heartbeat of humanity in tune with Mother Nature.***

# The Waiting Game

It was the start of the dark period on Earth and the king of negative energy, Ravan, called all his apprentices together. He wanted to ensure everyone was on the same page and able to perform their role of darkness.

"There's no room for complacency," Ravan warned. "You will all be spending lots of time on earth among the humans and our job is to make sure they never find God. We have to make sure they do not remember the Supreme Being or the divine virtues hidden within them."

"Some of you will remember how it goes. Every cycle, we get to play our part late in the game. They all have a beautiful time during the light phase, now it's our turn. Our job is to shatter this lovely world and make it hell!"

"Just as their spiritual power weakens, we will be ready. They are in the seeking phase, looking everywhere for the source of their own strength. This is when they start thinking about God and looking for the Divine in their memories and surroundings. They vaguely remember the time when they were happy and peaceful and will try to recreate it. It's our job to keep them weak, unhappy and peaceless and always searching. If we don't, we will lose the world to goodness again like we do every cycle, and I don't want it to happen again!" proclaimed Ravan.

There was a long silence as the seriousness of Raven's message sank in. His apprentices waited to hear his plan for what to do this time. But Ravan read their minds and demanded they provide a plan.

"So, what are you going to do about it this time? Any bright ideas?"

The apprentices were silent, scratching their heads and furrowing their brows and not offering any suggestions! "Come on," said Ravan, "we don't have forever, we have to get on this right away!"

Very tentatively a young apprentice raised his hand: "Sir we could tell them straight up there is no God and they should just forget the whole idea of a Supreme Being."

"Nice try," said Ravan, "but that won't work. Part of the deal is that God hides the memory of Him and the divine virtues in their hearts and it always attracts them back to God. That slim memory is buried deep within them. They often can't name it or even admit it's there but sooner or later some of them have a moment when they know God exists. We'll have to do better than that!"

Crestfallen the apprentice sat down. Another brave little apprentice raised his arm, "Sir, we could tell them there is no such thing as sin or wrong-doing and they have nothing to fear. We can tell them Hell is just a myth."

"Sorry to disappoint you." said Ravan, but those very same divine virtues hidden deep in their hearts, will alert them when they are going off course. Their conscience will poke them. Somehow, they have enough strength left to know that when they stop listening to their inner voice, terrible things happen. They remember how bad it gets and how awful hell on earth feels. You'll have to think harder if we are to defeat goodness!"

A third apprentice puts up his hand and slowly and thoughtfully began, "Well, as you say, there's no good in telling them there is no God, they all have the virtues buried in their hearts; and there's no good telling them that there's no such thing as sin or Hell. What if we told them, there was no hurry!"

Ravan was delighted. "Brilliant," he squealed. "That's exactly what we'll do. You'll go far young man. Well done."

And so, it came to be that humans carried on believing in God and knowing about sin, but never doing much about it, because after all, there was no hurry.

*When I promise something for the future, I postpone the opportunity to give in the present moment. As life unfolds, events may prevent me from giving at the 'promised' time, despite my deep integrity and commitment. When I approach each moment as the only certain moment to give, then I will give now and not delay. We have the moment in front of us to make the most with.*

***The time is now!***

# Unity is Strength

Long ago there was an old farmer living in the village who owned many properties. He looked after these properties very well and became quite rich and lived a happy life with his four sons. However, as they grew older the boys began to quarrel among themselves. The farmer advised them to be friendly, but they did not listen, and he became very sad. *How can I teach them to be good to each other they are always quarreling? I must put an end to this he thought.*

The farmer was always thinking about his quarreling children, and this affected his health, and he became very ill. When he felt he was about to die, he called all his sons to his bedside, "Children, you must not quarrel."

He asked a servant to bring a bundle of sticks which were then tied together. He then gave each of his sons the bundle in turn asking them to break it, each tried to do so but all of them failed.

He then asked the servant to untie the bundle, and he gave each one of his sons one of the sticks. Again, he ordered each one to break the stick. Each of them broke the stick easily.

The father then said to his sons, "You see children you are not able to break the sticks when they are tied together as a bundle. Do you know why? Because when they are joined together, they are strong. The reason you could break them when separated is because they were divided. So do not quarrel and instead, be strongly united."

*They say there is no 'I' in team. But there IS an 'I' in unity. The belief that I must lose myself to become part of a team is a false belief. It leads to subtle forms of oppression and cloning. We are each unique and different. Unity is created when there is an appreciation of the uniqueness of each member of the team and a willingness to combine strengths to achieve a shared outcome. A strong sense of self-respect is the basis of true unity.*

***We are stronger together than apart.***

# The Long Ladle

In ancient times a disciple asked his guru, "I would like to know what heaven is like."

The guru through his mystical powers immediately brought in front of him a scene of a house with two doors. He opened one of the doors and the disciple looked in.

In the middle of the room, was a large round table. In the middle of the table was a large round pot of stew which smelled delicious.

The people sitting around were thin and they looked famished. They were holding spoons with long handles. They were able to reach into the pot of stew and take a spoonful, but because the handles were longer than their arms, they could not get the spoon back into their mouth.

The disciple shuddered at the sight of this misery and suffering.

The guru said, "Now you have seen Hell".

They went to the next room and opened the door. It was the same as the first one. There was the large round table with the large pot of stew. The people were equipped with the same long handled spoons, but the people were nourished and plump, and were laughing and talking.

"This is Heaven," the holy man said.

"I do not understand," said the disciple.

"It is simple," said the guru. "It requires one skill. You see they have learned to feed each other, while the greedy think only of themselves."

*"Hell is where you have to tolerate that which is intolerable." Charles Eisenstein*

*We can think of heaven and hell as descriptions of the quality of life on earth. Heaven can be seen as the ideal state of humanity in harmonious relationship with Mother Nature, animals, and each other. Hell is a time when all suffer. Even the wealthy suffer from fear, anxiety, and loneliness. Trying to fix hell is a BIG job and may not be possible. But creating heaven is a minute-to-minute contribution of high-quality energy such as cooperation and peace.*

***Together, we can.***

# It's Time

"Children? How can we trust children with this mission? They are so unreliable."

The Keeper of the Earth stood in front of the arched window at one end of the Council Room, considering this sudden twist of events. He stood as if on watch, a stance he had held for all time. His face, chiseled like granite, held unyielding stony grey eyes. White hair fell down his back like snow covering the Himalayas. His cape was iridescent, shimmering with mineral flecks of gold, copper and zinc.

"I know it is hard to believe, but they are the only ones who can do it," the Keeper of the Water soothed.

Her flowing appearance was a stark contrast to his fixed demeanor. As she moved, her aquamarine cape rippled around her like ocean waves. The fringe was as white and fluffy as sea foam and floated across the surface of the floor as she walked to the window to stand beside her old friend.

"Because humans are destroying it, they must be the ones to restore it," the Keeper of the Air offered breezily. The room freshened; her ethereal presence was felt more than seen.

"But why children?" blazed the Keeper of the Fire. "Surely there are more qualified candidates among the human race."

Mother Nature could not hold on much longer. The destruction of the mountains for minerals, the forests for wood and the soil for agribusiness had weakened the Earth. The extraction of oil from beneath its crust had left the Earth pockmarked and depleted. Trillions of tons of human waste and radioactive material thrown into the once sparkling ocean had poisoned Water. Earthquakes were common as Fire's magma shifted tectonic plates. The planet's protective ozone layer had been so weakened that the fire of the sun scorched the land. Air was contaminated with cancer causing toxins, and carbon dioxide emissions were making the air unbreathable in many parts of the world. Plant and animal species were becoming extinct. Life on the planet was perilously out of balance.

Human beings fought greedily for shrinking resources and struggled to survive. Having lost the truth of their natural state they no longer lived in harmony with nature, themselves or each other.

The Divine Power, the Overseer of all things physical and metaphysical, had explained. "Mother

Nature has called you together to prepare for the regeneration process." His presence was invisible, and his voice was a whisper, but it filled the room with power.

"Although you know the planet will never be destroyed," he continued, "the time of harmonious living has ended. The footprints of billions have worn Nature to her lowest state."

The Keepers had watched over the years as successive attempts to regenerate the world had failed. Humans lost energy or became disheartened and frustrated with each other. The result was war. Eventually people gave up. Lulled into a state of coping, they accepted this degraded state as normal.

Anxious as the Keepers were to restore balance, they were told they must await the results of a mission that would determine the fate of the human race.

"Some humans sense the need for change, but they do not understand that the planet requires regeneration on an unprecedented scale," said the Keeper of the Earth. "How can children possibly comprehend what is required?"

"The children still believe in a better world." The Keeper of the Air's lilting voice was like a breeze as it wafted through the room. "Their faith in the future is the last remaining trace of humanity's original pure nature. Their optimism will motivate them and protect them and give them the power they need to keep going when they are challenged."

"Excellent. I'm ready now," flamed the Keeper of the Fire. He savoured the thought of hot lava renewing the soil.

The Keeper of the Water hesitated, knowing she would have to cover the earth to cleanse it. "I will be ready when it's time," she said quietly.

"Fine," conceded the Keeper of the Earth finally. "How will we know which children to choose? There are so many of them."

"I have been looking." The voice of the Divine Power was quiet and final. "I have found them."

*From Seven Secrets of the Universe by Judy Johnson*

---

*Faith in the future of a better world comes from a place of optimism. Hope awaits on the other side of despair. Hope is not something that I have. Hope is something that I create with my actions. Each step I take in a positive direction builds an inner flame of hope ~ until a lamp of hope is visible in me. Hope is contagious. When others see this light in me, they become hopeful also.*

**_We are the ones we have been looking for._**

# Editors' Note

*We hope you have had as much fun reading these stories as we had assembling them. Hopefully they have enriched your experience of yourself and your life.*

*Likely some of the stories resonated more with you than others. You may wish to reflect on the reason for this. Perhaps they reminded you of something close to your heart or reflected your lived experience.*

*Stories are mirrors for the soul.*

*Live well, live close to yourself, meditate always!!*

*With love,*

*Judy, Carol, Teri, Sheila*

*Halifax Brahma Kumaris Centre*

# Some Background

- The Brahma Kumaris are a spiritual movement that originated in Hyderabad, Sindh, during the 1930s. The movement has distinguished itself from its Hindu roots and sees itself as a vehicle for spiritual teaching rather than as a religion.
- Over 8000 Meditation Centres in 125 countries-organization run by donation only.
- It is the largest spiritual movement led by women.
- An NGO with General Consultative Status with the United Nations Economic and Social Council.
- Purpose of the movement: to create a more peaceful world, one person at a time. The slogan is: *as I change, the world changes.*
- BK teaches a form of meditation called Raja Yoga that focuses on soul consciousness or the construct that our primary identity is that we're souls who live in bodies. In meditation we aim to connect to our inherent soul qualities: bliss, love, peace, power, purity.
- The Brahma Kumaris is oriented to service work worldwide in many forms: featuring many online and in person courses, retreats, etc. all free of charge.

- Philosophies for living are grounded in a sustainable approach to the environment and human relationships over the long term for the planet. Living lightly on the planet and the idea that when we feel fulfilled, people will naturally be inclined "take-less" materially, from the environment and from one another.
- The main Spiritual University Campus in India has capacity for 25,000 students which can all be fed 3 meals a day powered solely by solar generation.
- There is IQ, EQ, and SQ (spiritual intelligence) ~ SQ is what the BKs are about: teaching people how to become masters of their state of mind and how one can sustain their inherently enthusiastic, loving human spirit.

www.ingramcontent.com/pod-product-compliance
Lightning Source LLC
LaVergne TN
LVHW091214150826
845672LV00005B/1355

* 9 7 9 8 8 9 6 3 2 6 9 8 4 *